THE ULTIMATE AT-HOME

ACTIVITY GUIDE

mike LOWERY

putnam

G. P. Putnam's Sons

This book is dedicated
to my wife, Katrin.

The reason that this book exists is because of
Katrin (the *SAME* Katrin from up there!). She's my
wife and partner and the reason I've (somewhat)
kept my sanity during all of these strange months
spent at home. Her projects with the kids always
turn out great, and she doesn't get mad when I
accidentally microwave the wrong soap and we all
have to go out on the lawn for an hour while the
smoke clears. Anyway, thank you, Katrin.

G. P. Putnam's Sons
An imprint of Penguin Random House LLC, New York

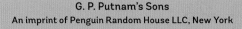

G. P. Putnam's Sons is a registered trademark of Penguin Random House LLC.

Visit us online at penguinrandomhouse.com

Library of Congress Cataloging-in-Publication Data is available.

Manufactured in China by RR Donnelley Asia Printing Solutions Ltd.
ISBN 9780593326091
1 3 5 7 9 10 8 6 4 2

Design by Eileen Savage. Text set in Andes Rounded.
Hand lettering by Mike Lowery.
The illustrations in this book were rendered using
a variety of digital techniques.

A NOTE FROM THE AUTHOR

(a message to the adults)

Keeping the kids entertained at home can be challenging sometimes. The toys are boring, they have read all the books, their friends are busy, and you don't want them to watch that one movie with the annoying song over and over again. When you can't think of anything fun to do and you need a little creative input to find a way to spend time with everyone, pull out this book!

This book is a collection of some of my family's favorite activities to break up the daily routine. It's full of ways to get moving, connect with nature, show off your creative side, and hang out with friends and family—even when they're in another town! Some of these projects and suggestions are one-time activities, but some of them might become favorites that you do again and again. I tried to stick to activities with materials that you might have around the house, but in some cases, you'll need to pick up a few things to complete the project.

Sometimes we just need a little push to get us moving, and the following pages are meant to be just that. The activities are just suggestions and are meant to be changed and adapted to fit *your* family or group. You can add your own twist to really make the ideas yours!

—MIKE

CONTENTS

Key to Important Icons in the Book

 ADULT SUPERVISION

SOME of these activities require ADULT SUPERVISION! I know, I know . . . you're a supersmart kid and you're going to be extra careful, BUT when you see this icon, it means you'll need an adult's help with one or more of the steps, so they should be present for the full project.

 MESSY

This icon indicates that the activity can get pretty messy, and I recommend using EXTREME care to protect clothing, surface areas, and sometimes skin. Use gloves when using dyes and ink. That rug might not mean much to you, but I'm CERTAIN the adult in your house wouldn't love you making any colorful alterations to it.

 **INTERNET NEEDED**

This icon indicates that the activity will require a tablet, smartphone, or computer with internet access.

HEY!
Read this before
you get started!

Introduction

**Here's some
(maybe-a-little-boring-but-super-important)
stuff you need to know!**

1. **MOST** of the projects in this book require ADULT PERMISSION. Just double-check that it's okay with an adult before you get started.

2. **LOTS** of the activities in this book will require a few common art supplies. Try to keep these items handy: tape, glue (typically school glue, but a glue stick is useful, too!), a ruler, scissors, a hobby knife, something to draw with (pens, pencils), something to color with (paint, markers, crayons), paper and construction paper, twine, and googly eyes (just kidding—those aren't required, but they're definitely a lot of fun to play with!). However, some projects will require specific materials or ingredients that you may not have at home but are easy to find.

3. Read through EACH STEP carefully before starting any activity!

A note about eco-friendly crafting: It's important that we keep our planet in mind, even when we are crafting. Try to reuse materials instead of going out and getting new supplies, and avoid toxic paints that aren't good for your skin OR the environment. Try to avoid a lot of waste, and recycle any scraps.

A note about glitter: Throughout the book, there are many projects that you can add glitter to. I don't personally like to use it because it's really messy! It's also not great for the environment. (It's made up of tiny little pieces of plastic that end up in the ocean, where it can be eaten by little fish.)

MAKE STUFF!

Comics!
Glow-in-the-dark chalk!
Slime!

This section is full of ideas for awesome things you can make!

MAKE A FLIP-BOOK

WHAT YOU NEED:

PENCIL · HEAVY PAPER · SCISSORS · BINDER CLIP

1. Cut your heavy paper into twenty to forty 3 x 5 inch rectangles. You can also use index cards and skip the cutting part.

2. Let's start reeeeeally simple for our first flip-book. Draw a very easy-to-draw object on one card. (One idea is a frog that will open and close its mouth.)

3 Place your next sheet of paper over the first one and hold both up to a window. The light will let you see your first drawing. On your second sheet, trace the image, but slightly shift the part you want to move when the pages flip. Repeat this process with all of your sheets of paper.

 LIKE THIS:

1   2   3   4

4 Use the binder clip to hold the pages together. Flip the pages with your thumb, and **TA-DA!**

You've made your first movie. Now try to make one that's a little more complicated!

DIG DEEPER

If you liked making a paper flip-book, you can try making one online. There are a lot of really great, easy flip-book apps.

Like in our paper flip-book, I recommend starting VERY simple. Try making a circle move across the screen. After you get the hang of it, try making a person wave or something more complicated (like an alien eating pizza)!

SEE ONE IN **ACTION!**

LIKE THIS

FLIP HERE

DRAW A COMIC
ABOUT THE BEST TRIP YOU'VE {EVER} TAKEN!

A FEW TIPS:

1 Go through photos of the trip to help you remember things that happened.

2 Think about why you liked the trip and try showing that in your comic. Did you make a new friend? Did you try new foods? Did you get soaked in all of your clothes while unexpectedly getting caught in a rainstorm?! These would all be great things to include in your comic.

3 Draw little squares and fill them with fun/awesome/ crazy things from the trip.

4 This is YOUR story, so have FUN with it!

FAMILY DISCUSSION: Ask everyone to describe their most favorite vacation. Then ask them to tell the story of their funniest or weirdest family vacation moment.

START A DAILY JOURNAL

Any day is a GREAT day to start keeping a daily journal. Journaling can help you keep track of things that you did and your ideas. All you need is a notebook, and it doesn't need to be fancy. A simple spiral-bound book or even stapled-together paper works just fine.

NOTE: You're also allowed to draw in it! Draw what you ate! Draw your friends! Draw a smiley face if you're feeling happy or a frowny face if today wasn't the best.

Be sure to write down the date, and try to make it a goal to write something in it every day.

MONDAY 14TH
I ATE
TODAY I FEEL

ANOTHER FUN IDEA! Come up with a funny character and write some journal entries from their point of view. What would a sloth write in their diary? "Dear Diary, Today I ate one leaf. It took me 8 hours. Now I'm sleepy."

Not sure what to write about? Here are a few ideas.

- How do you feel?
- What did you eat?
- Did anything funny happen today?
- What is the weather like?
- What is something new you learned today?

- Did anyone in your family do something silly?
- What was the best and worst part of your day?
- What are you thankful for?
- Where would you like to be right now?

MAKE GLOW·IN·THE DARK CHALK

There's no better way to draw a nighttime masterpiece than with GLOWING sidewalk chalk!

What you'll need:

- A paper or plastic cup for mixing
- Water-based glow-in-the-dark paint
- Water
- 1 cup plaster of paris
- Plastic ice cube tray

Steps:

1. Pour 2 tablespoons of your paint into the cup.

2. Add 2 tablespoons of water.

3. Stir it up!

4. Add some of the plaster of paris until it starts to thicken and becomes tough to mix anymore.

5. Scoop it out and squish it into the ice cube sections. You probably won't have enough to fill up the whole tray, so just fill up as many squares as you can.

6. Let it completely dry. This can take a few days!

7. Make some art! I'm sure you'll receive GLOWING reviews!

HEY! Always ask an adult where you are allowed to draw.

TIE-DYE A SHIRT

What you'll need:

- Tie-dye kit from the craft store
- A clean 100% cotton T-shirt (white works best)
- Rubber bands
- Plastic or rubber gloves
- Plastic bag

Steps:

1. Follow the directions to mix the ink!

2. Decide what pattern you want (look online for lots of ideas). You can twist up your shirt and make cool patterns.

3. Be sure to wear gloves! Put the ink on the shirt to get the pattern you want.

4. Put the shirt in a plastic bag overnight.

5. Wash your new shirt BY ITSELF in the washing machine (actually, maybe wash it a few times before you wash it with any other clothes, just in case there's any extra dye that's DYE-ing to get on your other clothes!).

6. Put on your shirt, grow out a lonnggg beard, and go listen to "California Dreamin'" by the Mamas & the Papas.

MAKE A LAVA LAMP

Since we already made a tie-dyed shirt, we might as well make a lava lamp to go with it, right?

What you'll need:

- Empty 2-liter plastic bottle with the label removed
- 3 cups vegetable oil
- Water
- Food coloring
- 2 sodium bicarbonate tablets (aka Alka-Seltzer tablets!)

Try shining a flashlight on the bottle for a fun light show.

Steps:

1. Fill the bottle $\frac{1}{3}$ of the way with vegetable oil.

2. Fill the rest of the bottle with tap water.

3. Add a few drops of food coloring.

4. Break the sodium bicarbonate tablets into small pieces and put them in the bottle.

5. When the tablets are dissolved, put the cap on and shake the bottle slowly until the oil forms large blobs.

MAKE CLAY

What you'll need:

- 2 cups salt
- ⅔ cup room-temperature water
- 1 cup cornstarch
- ½ cup cold water
- Medium-sized pot
- Food coloring (optional)

Steps:

1. Pour the salt and the room-temperature water into the pot. Heat on medium for 5 minutes while stirring.

2. Take the pot off the stove and stir in the cornstarch and the cold water. Mix until you've gotten rid of all of the clumps. No clumps allowed!

3. Return the pot to the stove. Heat the mixture on medium until it thickens.

4. Let it cool.

5. Once it's cool enough to touch, you can mold it into any shape you want.

6. Let it dry and your tiny sculpture will harden.

7. Now you can paint or decorate it any way you'd like! Draw on it! Add googly eyes!

ADD GOOGLY EYES!

CAN YOU MAKE...

A CAT?

A DINO?

AN ICE CREAM?

DESIGN YOUR OWN BAND SHIRT

Got a great idea for a totally imaginary up-and-coming band or musician? Maybe it's a band of bats that play synthesizers? Maybe it's a singing Icelandic pony named Guðrún?

What you'll need:

- An old T-shirt (light colors work best)
- Fabric markers or iron-on transfers (see explanation below)

Steps:

1. Decide on the name of your band.

2. Design some cool lettering. Add a pattern or images to make a logo.

3. Get the design onto the shirt with:

   a. Fabric markers. These are an easy way to draw your idea on a shirt. Don't forget to add the tour locations and dates on the back! (Steps vary brand-to-brand, so follow the instructions on your pens or fabric paint for applying and drying the ink or paint.)

   b. Iron-on transfers. If you've got an inkjet printer at home, you can buy special paper that will let you transfer a design from your computer to a shirt!

   c. If you're feeling REALLY adventurous, there are a few print-on-demand companies online that will let you buy a few shirts that have your custom design.

ANOTHER FUN IDEA!
Your shirt doesn't have to be for a band! Design a shirt for yourself. Think about an image or icon that you would like to wear on a T-shirt, or make one for a friend.

MAKE SOAP CLOUDS

If it's a rainy day *outside*, why not make some nice, fluffy clouds *inside*? This is an easy one.

What you'll need:

- Kitchen parchment paper or paper plates
- Microwave
- Bar of Ivory soap (this just works the best)

ANOTHER FUN IDEA!
Use cookie cutters to cut the foamy cloud into shapes.

Steps:

1. Cut a sheet of the parchment paper to cover the inside bottom of your microwave. Microwave-safe paper plates work, too.

2. Microwave the soap for two minutes. Watch as the soap totally transforms into a magical puffball. Why is it doing this? There's water in the soap, and as the water evaporates, it makes bubbles and the soap expands.

Now for the fun part! Take the whole thing into the bath with you!

CREATE INSTRUMENTS

There are all kinds of great musical instruments that are easy to make at home. Here are a few examples.

TIN CAN DRUM

BALLOON

RUBBER BAND

TIN CAN

What you'll need:

- Balloon
- Scissors
- Empty can or jelly jar
- Rubber bands
- Small sticks (like chopsticks)

CAREFUL: Metal cans can be sharp on top. Take care not to cut your fingers.

Steps:

1. Cut off the neck of a balloon.

2. Stretch the top of the balloon over the open end of the can. Secure it with a rubber band.

3. Use a chopstick (or any kind of small stick) to beat on the drum!

4. Use different-sized cans to see how it changes the sound of the drums. You can also fill your drum with dry lentils and shhhhake it.

(If you used a jelly jar, you are ready for your JAM SESSION.)

SHOEBOX GUITAR

BOX

CARD- BOARD TRIANGLE

RUBBER BANDS

PAPER FASTENERS

What you'll need:

- A shoebox or other small box
- Scissors
- Rubber bands (mix of widths)
- Paper fasteners
- Piece of cardstock paper OR small scrap of thin cardboard

Steps:

1. Take the lid off of your shoebox and cut a round hole in the middle.

2. Cut the rubber bands.

3. Tightly stretch the rubber bands over the hole in the lid and secure them to the edge of the lid with the paper fasteners.

4. Cut a small rectangle of cardboard and fold it into a triangle.

5. Slide this under one end of the rubber bands.

6. You can decorate the outside of the box however you'd like!

7. Now you're ready to ROCK.

FAMILY DISCUSSION: Does anyone in your family play an instrument? Find out when they started learning how to play. Ask what instrument everyone would want to learn and what kind of music they'd want to play.

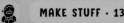

MAKE CARDS FOR
WEIRD (AND TOTALLY REAL) HOLIDAYS

Sure, you know about Halloween and Mother's Day, but did you know there's a holiday called Hug Your Cat Day (June 4) where you celebrate by . . . hugging your cat? Are you more of a puppy lover? Well, don't worry, because April 10 is Hug Your Dog Day!

There are TONS of weird holidays. Some are official, some aren't, but they're all FUN. So let's join in the fun by making a greeting card for someone that shows off our love for these strange days.

NATIONAL HAT DAY! (JANUARY 15)

WORLD PARTY DAY! (APRIL 3)

NATIONAL GRILLED CHEESE DAY! (APRIL 12)

PIZZA PARTY DAY! (MAY 15)

HAMBURGER DAY! (MAY 28)

WORLD UFO DAY! (JULY 2)

NATIONAL BEARD DAY! SEPTEMBER 3

TALK LIKE A PIRATE DAY SEPTEMBER 19

A FEW TIPS:

- Look up "weird holiday" and find one that is coming up that sounds like it would be fun or interesting to draw. Look to see what holidays fall on your birthday or the birthday of the recipient.

- Use a sheet of thick paper (like construction paper or card stock). Fold it in half like a greeting card.

- Can't think of what to draw? You can just hand-letter the name of the holiday!

LET'S MAKE SLIME

Slime is the ULTIMATE at-home activity! It's fun to make and just as fun to play with, and it's really easy.

When you're done playing with your slime, keep it stored in an airtight container.

HERE'S WHAT YOU'LL NEED:

8OZ SCHOOL GLUE (x2)

FOOD COLORING (3 DROPS)

1 TEASPOON BAKING SODA

2 TABLESPOONS CONTACT LENS SOLUTION

Steps:

1. Squeeze both bottles of glue into a bowl and mix in a few drops of food coloring.

2. Mix in the baking soda. Stir until smooth.

3. Add the contact lens solution and mix.

4. When it starts to ball up, take it out and work it in your hands.

5. After kneading it by hand, if it's still sticky, add a little more of the contact lens solution.

SEND A POSTCARD FROM AN **EXOTIC** LOCATION

...IN YOUR HOUSE!

GREETINGS FROM THE KITCHEN

HOME

HELLO FROM THE BACKYARD!

THE BACK:

STAMP

YOUR ADDRESS

YOUR NOTE

RECIPIENT'S ADDRESS

You don't need to be on an adventure far from home to drop a postcard in the mail! Send one from an exotic location . . . in your home.

Cut a piece of heavy card stock into a rectangle (4½ x 6 inches works great) and make a postcard to tell a friend or family member about an exciting place in your house or yard. Come up with a fun tagline for your favorite spot, or look up designs of old vacation postcards and copy them.

Don't forget to add your name, your address, the recipient's address, and a stamp before you put it in the mailbox.

MAKE A MARSHMALLOW CATAPULT

Protect your castle from enemies with this totally sweet marshmallow launcher.

What you'll need:

- 9 craft (or Popsicle) sticks
- Rubber bands
- Plastic spoon
- Marshmallows (of course!)

Steps:

1. Make a stack of 7 craft sticks and wrap 2 rubber bands tightly around the ends.

2. Stack 2 craft sticks and wrap a rubber band around one end.

3. Split the 2 sticks and place the stack of 7 in the middle (in a plus-sign shape).

4. Add rubber bands in an X shape to secure the intersection of the sticks.

5. Tape a plastic spoon to the top craft stick.

6. Place a marshmallow in the spoon, pull it back, and WOOSH!

SCIENTIFIC NOTE! You just made a simple machine. This catapult is actually a type of lever.

TIP: Have one person launch and another person try and catch them in their mouth.

— SPOON

TAPE

CRAFT STICKS

RUBBER BANDS

MAKE FINGER PUPPETS

What you'll need:

- Sheets of felt or colored paper
- Glue
- Googly eyes, yarn, buttons . . . (optional)

Steps:

1. Cut 2 large thumb shapes out of the felt or paper that are exactly the same size.

2. Glue the long edges and tips together, but leave the bottom side open.

3. Cut a large circle shape for a face and decorate.

4. Glue the face to the tip of the finger.

GLUE HERE

LEAVE OPEN

HELLO!

Who is this going to be? A person, an animal, or a monster? It's up to you. Add hair using yarn, cut out a hat or some ears . . .

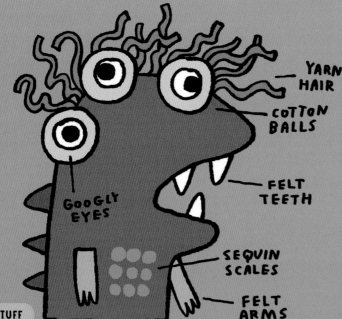

YARN HAIR

COTTON BALLS

FELT TEETH

GOOGLY EYES

SEQUIN SCALES

FELT ARMS

MAKE A SOCK MONSTER

Glue eyes, arms, hair, horns, and other fun stuff to your sock monster!

DESIGN A CARDBOARD TOWN

Cardboard is an excellent material to use for crafts, because it's strong but still easy to cut and glue together. You could build a playhouse out of it . . . or even an entire little town! The options are unlimited! What else can you come up with? Can you build a car or a space station?!

OTHER FUN IDEAS!

What you'll need:

- Cardboard boxes: Next time a grown-up orders some boring stuff from the internet (like socks or a toaster), make sure to save the box.
- Paper towels, toilet paper, and wrapping paper tubes
- Junk mail: Some junk mail is made from awesome thick paper that can come in handy.
- Glue
- Scissors
- Paint

Use your supplies to cut, glue, and decorate your own little town!

Experiment with your own designs. What shops are in your town? What kind of amazing house would you like to live in?

MAKE A STAMP

What you'll need:

- Craft foam (get the adhesive sheets if you can find them!)
- Cardboard
- Hobby knife (Only if you're really careful! Scissors work, too.)
- Paper
- Acrylic paint (if you want to print on fabric, then use fabric paint)
- Small plate
- Paintbrush (a foam brush works great)
- Permanent marker

Steps:

1. Use the permanent marker to draw a simple shape on the foam or cardboard.

2. Carefully cut it out.

3. If you're using foam, glue it to something sturdy, like a piece of cardboard.

4. Glue a stack of smaller pieces of cardboard to the back of the shape (to make it easier to pick up when you're stamping).

5. Use the brush to paint a very thin layer of paint on the foam or cardboard shape.

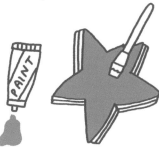

6. Push it hard against the surface of the paper you're printing on.

MAKE A STYROFOAM RELIEF PRINT

NOTE: It's best to reuse Styrofoam rather than going out and buying some. I recommend reusing the sheets that come with some fruits and veggies at the grocery store.

What you'll need:

- Styrofoam sheet (see NOTE)
- Pencil
- Acrylic paint
- Parchment paper or a paper plate
- An ink brayer (aka a paint roller—these are found at any art supply store)
- Paper

Steps:

1. Carefully draw on the bottom of the Styrofoam with a pencil. (You want to make an impression but not break all the way through.)

2. Squirt a small amount of acrylic paint on the parchment paper or plate.

3. Roll the brayer in the paint until it's covered all around.

4. Roll a thin layer of paint on the bottom of the Styrofoam.

5. Turn it over and push it hard against the paper. Lift up to reveal your print.

ANOTHER FUN IDEA! If you loved these printmaking techniques and you're ready to handle something a little bit more complicated, try a rubber-stamping kit. They come with a sheet of rubber, a cutter, ink, and some small tools that help with printing. They're harder to cut, but you can create much more complicated designs. You can find complete kits at art supply stores.

MAKE A PAPIER-MÂCHÉ PARTY ANIMAL

What you'll need:

- 1 cup water
- 1 cup flour
- A balloon
- Newspaper
- Tissue paper

Optional:

- String (twine is great)
- Candy!

ANOTHER FUN IDEA!

Turn this into a piñata.

1. Cut a small door near the top.
2. Carefully pop the balloon inside.
3. Fill it with candy, then tape the opening shut.
4. Attach twine to the top.
5. Hang it up and take turns hitting it with a stick until it breaks open!

Steps:

1. Mix the water with the flour to make paste.
2. Blow up the balloon.
3. Tear up strips of newspaper and dip them fully into the paste. Try to squeeze off any extra water.
4. Wrap the strips around the balloon and cover it fully. Repeat this process until you have several layers of newspaper covering the balloon.
5. Let it dry for at least one full day!
6. Decorate! What is this going to be? An owl, a cat, a face, or an alien? You can glue strips of tissue paper to it, paint it, draw on it . . . whatever you'd like!

PAPER STRIPS

BALLOON

CONSTRUCTION PAPER

MAKE A PENNANT BANNER

There's no need to wait for a special occasion to make a pennant banner. You can make one just to let someone in your family know how awesome they are!

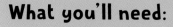

What you'll need:
- Twine
- Scissors
- Tape
- Colored or white paper

SOME OPTIONS:

"MOM IS COOL"
"LET'S PARTY!"

Steps:

1. Cut a large paper triangle for every letter that will go on your banner. They should all be the same size.

2. Write one letter on each triangle sheet with the short side as the top.

3. Poke holes in the top corners and run the string through, or attach with tape or glue.

4. Hang using tape!

MAKE SPY STUFF

You have been selected to be a special agent. Here are a few spy tools that will help you with your secret mission!

INVISIBLE INK

A classic spy tool to write secret messages to other agents!

What you'll need:

- Paper
- Cotton swab
- Blow dryer
- 1 lemon

Steps:

1. Cut the lemon in half and squeeze the juice into a small cup.

2. Dip the cotton swab in the juice and use it to write your secret message on the paper.

3. Let it dry.

4. Once it's totally dry, give the paper to an adult, who can use the blow dryer to heat up the message to read it.

SCIENTIFIC NOTE!
The carbon in the lemon juice reacts to the heat and turns from clear to brown.

meet me at the OLD LIBRARY!

PERISCOPE

See what's going on around the corner! Usually, periscopes only poke out of the top of submarines, but you can make your own sneaky peeking device!

What you'll need:

- Empty and clean milk carton
- Two small same-sized mirrors
- Hobby knife
- Tape

ANOTHER FUN IDEA!

Once you've mastered this small periscope, try making a really long one! You can use cardboard to make a long rectangular tube and cut flaps for the mirrors at both ends!

Steps:

1. Cut a hole on one side of the top of the carton and tape the mirror inside.

2. Cut a small window at the bottom of the carton. Leave the bottom edge attached.

3. Tape the mirror to it and adjust the flap until you can see the reflection in the mirror that's attached to the top of the carton.

4. Tape the flap and the mirror in place.

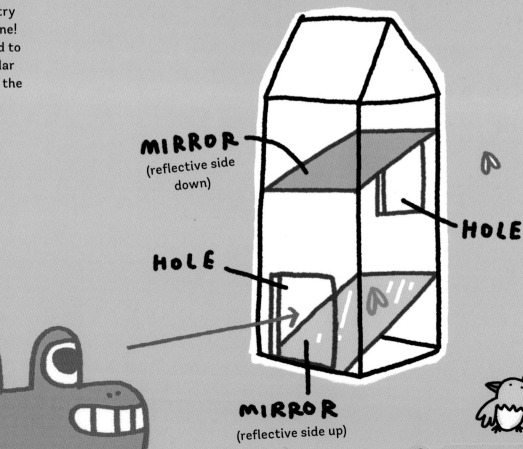

MIRROR (reflective side down)

HOLE

HOLE

MIRROR (reflective side up)

CIPHER WHEEL

A cipher is a secret way of coding a message. This cipher wheel can help you quickly send secret messages to other agents. It's also easy to change the code just in case your messages ever get intercepted!

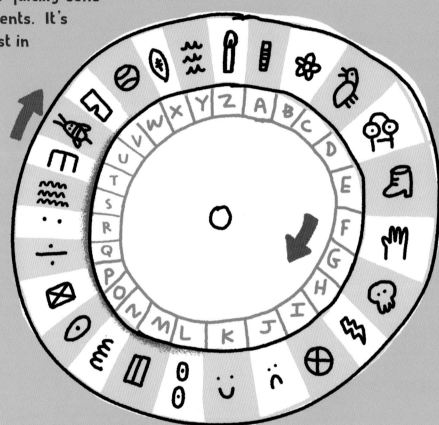

What you'll need:

- 2 sheets of heavy paper
- Paper fastener
- Markers
- Scissors

Steps:

1. Cut 2 circles out of the heavy paper. One should be ½ inch smaller than the other.

2. Push the paper fastener through the center of both circles.

3. Write the alphabet in a circle around the edge of the inner circle.

4. Draw 26 different easy-to-draw shapes around the edge of the outer circle right next to each letter. They can be silly faces or whatever you'd like!

Write a message using the shapes on the outside ring. Be sure to write at the top of the message what **A** equals so that your partner knows where the code begins!

Before you hand over the message and cipher wheel, turn the outer ring so it doesn't line up with the letters you used for your message.

CAN YOU DECODE THIS SECRET MESSAGE?

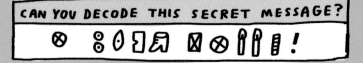

BOOK SAFE

What you'll need:

- An old hardcover book (you must get an adult to approve of the book!)
- Hobby knife
- Ruler
- Pencil
- Glue stick

Steps:

1. Draw a rectangle on the first page of the book with a ruler and a pencil. Don't make it too close to the edge.

2. Have an adult cut the shape out of the interior pages of the book.

3. Use a glue stick to lightly glue the edges of the pages together (optional).

4. Hide your treasured possessions!

PUT YOUR SPY STUFF HERE

FUN FOOD!

Mug cakes!

Pizza art!

Seaweed potato chips!

This section is all about sweets, treats, and other stuff you eat. Kitchens are made to get messy—it's a sign of great food being made. Just remember to help clean up.

SUPER-QUICK MUG CAKE

YUM!

What you'll need:

- 2 tablespoons butter
- 4 tablespoons flour
- 2 tablespoons sugar
- ½ teaspoon baking powder
- 1 egg yolk
- 1 tablespoon milk
- ½ tablespoon vanilla extract
- Sprinkles or chocolate chips (optional)

Steps:

1. Melt the butter in the microwave (approximately 45 seconds).

2. Mix the flour, sugar, and baking powder in a large coffee mug.

3. Add the melted butter, egg yolk, milk, and vanilla.

4. Stir it up!

5. Add chocolate chips or sprinkles.

6. Microwave for 45 seconds. If it isn't firm, microwave for 20 more seconds and check again. Repeat if necessary.

ANOTHER FUN IDEA! Quick mug cake frosting!

1. Stir 2 tablespoons room temperature butter with a fork.

2. Mix in 3 tablespoons powdered sugar.

3. Mix in 1 teaspoon milk until it becomes smooth and ready to spread!

PIZZA ART

MOZZARELLA

BASIL

BLACK OLIVE

MUSHROOM

TOMATO

PEPPERONI

MEATBALL

BLACK OLIVE

BELL PEPPER

GREEN OLIVE

This is an easy one! Buy premade dough and make small, personal-sized pizzas. Spread marinara sauce and then GO CRAZY WITH THE TOPPINGS! Heap on the cheese! Make a face out of pepperoni and mushrooms! Make a pattern! Color block!

FAMILY DISCUSSION: What do you like on your pizza? What would be the WORST THING EVER to have on pizza?! What would you put on a dessert pizza?

MONSTER COOKIES

WARNING! THESE COOKIES ARE DANGEROUS-LY FUN!

ICING

ICE CREAM

What you'll need:

- Sugar cookie dough (easy to make at home, and even easier to buy)
- Food coloring gel

Steps:

1. Cut your cookie dough into weird shapes and bake according to the directions on your dough.

2. Use the food coloring gel to draw weird eyes and mouths on your cookies to create the sweetest monsters ever.

MAKE YOUR OWN RAISINS

BAKING SHEET

GRAPES

PARCHMENT PAPER

What you'll need:

- Parchment paper
- Baking sheet
- Seedless grapes

Steps:

1. Heat oven to 200 degrees Fahrenheit.

2. Lay a sheet of parchment paper on the baking sheet.

3. Spread the grapes out evenly, and then bake for about 4 hours. Be sure to check on them, since oven times may vary and you don't want totally dried-out, yucky raisins!

4. Allow to cool before eating.

DEEEE-LISH!

TOSS 'EM IN YOUR YOGURT OR OATMEAL. (OR STRAIGHT INTO YOUR MOUTH!)

CRAZY POTATO CHIPS TASTE TEST

This might be my favorite activity in this entire book! Have one person go out and buy five or six different types of potato chips. Look for an international grocery store to try varieties from all over the world. Only this person should know what flavors were purchased.

Have them set the chips out in bowls marked with a number.

Everyone tries the chips and guesses what flavor they are. Don't say your answers out loud! Write your guesses on a piece of paper, and when everyone is done writing, go around and share what you think each flavor is.

Would you try one of these totally real chip flavors from around the world?

- Shrimp cocktail (UK)
- Shrimp and wasabi (Japan)
- Dill pickle (USA)
- Ham (Argentina)
- Crab (USA)
- Seaweed (Japan)
- Ketchup (Canada)
- Smoked beef (South Africa)
- Salmon teriyaki (Indonesia)
- Maple bacon (USA)
- Blueberry (China)
- Caviar (Russia)

ANOTHER FUN IDEA! Try this same activity with:

- Fruits or veggies (Can you name them without seeing or touching them?)
- Juices
- Sodas
- Candy (Do this one blindfolded!)

ICE CREAM

Did you know that you can make your own amazing ice cream at home?!

What you'll need:

- Gallon-sized zipper freezer bag
- Ice
- 8 tablespoons salt
- ½ cup heavy cream
- ¼ teaspoon vanilla extract
- 2 tablespoons sugar
- Pint-sized zipper bag
- Sprinkles (optional—but also pretty important)

Steps:

1. Fill the gallon bag halfway with ice and then add the salt.
2. In a bowl, mix the cream, vanilla, and sugar really well.
3. Pour this liquid mixture into the pint bag and seal it tightly.
4. Now put the smaller bag into the larger bag and seal.
5. Shake it up for about 8 minutes.
6. Top with sprinkles!

ANOTHER FUN IDEA! Try mixing in fun stuff like fresh fruit or chocolate chips!

GET MOVING!

Everyone feels better when they move their bodies, and there are lots of fun ways to do it! This section is full of activities that will get your blood pumping!

FLY PAPER AIRPLANES

Have everyone in your family fold and decorate a paper airplane, then hold a competition to see whose flies the farthest.

Here's one way to make one, but there are TONS of different designs you can use.

① Fold a sheet of paper in half and unfold it.

② Fold down the corners like this:

③ Fold in half.

④ Fold one half down like this to make a wing . . .

⑤ . . . and now fold this side down to make the other wing.

⑥

DONE!

HAVE A PAPER AIRPLANE COMPETITION!

SEE WHOSE CAN CAN GO THE FARTHEST!

DO YOGA

Doing yoga is a great activity for the whole family. Doing yoga can help your brain and your body relax and get stronger.

Here are a few easy poses, but the best way to get started is to watch a video online with basic instructions.

DOWNWARD DOG!

BUTTERFLY POSE!

BOAT POSE!

TREE POSE!

SHOULDER STAND!

MAKE A TREASURE MAP

Hide a treasure somewhere in your house. Then, make a map with obstacles, and invite someone else to find it. When they've completed each step, they get the prize.

N
W E
S

1 Jump over the ferocious bear.

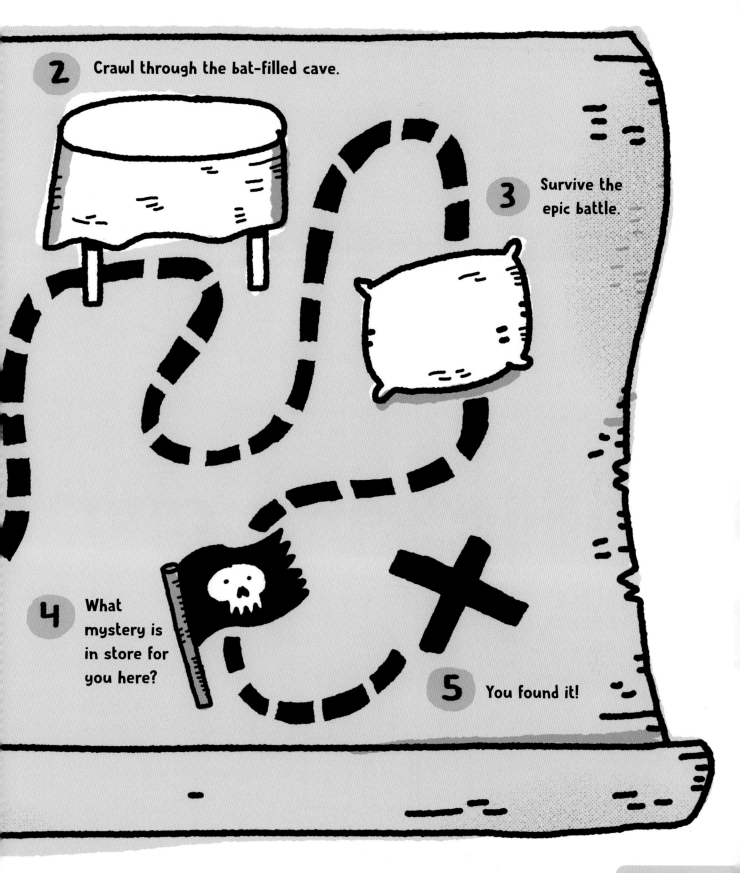

BOWL INDOORS

In your hallway, set up a few items that might be easy to knock over (like empty plastic bottles).

Use a medium-sized rubber ball like a bowling ball and try and knock over all of the pins!

If you knock them all over three times in a row, it's called a TURKEY!

ANOTHER FUN IDEA!

KNOCK DOWN CANS

Build a tower of empty (and clean!) cans like this:

Try and knock over as many as possible in one throw. If you don't have a ball, you can use a rolled-up-sock ball.

DESIGN A SIDEWALK OBSTACLE COURSE

START HERE

JUMP OVER THIS GUY!

BALANCE ON THIS LINE

SPIN 3 TIMES

HOP LIKE A BUNNY 5 TIMES!

WATCH OUT FOR PIRANHAS!

YOU MADE IT!

Make a fun challenge for neighbors who are out walking. Include instructions for all kinds of fun actions and see who participates.

HAVE A SILLY RACE

Here are a few options

Run with a balloon between your knees

Crab race

Run with an egg on a spoon (you should do this one outside!)

Run backwards

Jump on one leg

Walk with a book on your head

Tie two people's legs together

Hop like a rabbit

JUGGLE

Juggling isn't easy, but once you get the hang of it, it's very impressive! Start with three handkerchiefs or cloth napkins to get the motions down.

How to get started:

1. Toss one handkerchief from hand to hand in a wide arc.

2. Next, hold one handkerchief in each hand. Toss one toward the other in a high arc, and when it's at a height a little over your head, toss the second one to the other hand. Now practice this for a bit.

3. When you're ready to add in a third handkerchief, you might want to **DIG DEEPER** and find a good video that will walk you easily through the steps. Once you've got it down (again, it's not easy . . . give it time!), you can upgrade to beanbags or even juggling balls.

CREATE AN INDOOR OBSTACLE COURSE

Set up an obstacle course and time the contestants!

Here are some suggested obstacles:

① HULA-HOOP  FIVE TIMES

② CRAWL UNDER 3 CHAIRS

③ DO 5 JUMPING JACKS

④  THROW A BALL INTO A BASKET

⑤ BALANCE ON THIS YARN

⑥  STACK THE CUPS

⑦  HOP ACROSS THE PILLOWS

⑧  TAPE A PIECE OF STREAMER PAPER UP IN A HALL AS A FINISH LINE!

What else could you add to your obstacle course?

MAKE A "LASER" MAZE

String yarn, streamers, or twine throughout a room.

See who can get through fastest without pulling any of the string down.

GET SILLY!

Are you ready to giggle? This section will get you and the rest of your family laughing!

PUT ON A PUPPET SHOW

Put on a play for your family using your stuffed animals or finger puppets.

What you'll need:

- Hobby knife
- A large, three-paneled presentation board or a big cardboard box
- 1 yard of fabric (optional)
- Packing tape (optional)
- Twine or rope (optional)
- Your favorite art supplies
- Your favorite stuffed animals (or the sock puppets you made from page 18)

BACK VIEW

TAPE

CLOTH

STRING

CUT HOLE

FRONT VIEW

Steps:

1. Use the hobby knife to cut a large window in the board.

2. Optional: Cut the fabric in half and tape the two sections to the sides of the window. Use the twine to tie back the middle of the fabric. Now you have curtains!

3. Decorate the other side of the board like the outside of a puppet theater stage.

Don't forget the popcorn!

FAMILY DISCUSSION: If there was a TV show about your life, what would it be called? If you could be on any show, what would it be?

ANOTHER FUN IDEA! You could also build a TV out of a box and put on a TV show. Be the host of your own game show!

DRAW WITH YOUR EYES CLOSED!

NO PEEKING!

Give everyone some paper and a pencil. Suggest a topic for everyone to draw, but no peeking! Start with barnyard animals and then move on to a house, a car, or even a rocket ship.

BUNNY

ANOTHER FUN IDEA!

DRAW IN A MIRROR!

HMM.

MIRROR

PAPER

MAKE UP A
SILLY DANCE

Pick one of your favorite songs, make up a silly dance, and see if everyone can learn it. Video chat with Grandma, your aunt, or a friend, and see if they can learn it, too.

Come up with more!
Ask everyone in your family to show you their favorite dance move.

MAKE FUNNY HATS

Have a funny hat party using paper and all kinds of materials.

Roll paper into a cone. Tape ribbon or strips of tissue paper to the end for a homemade hennin (that's a princess hat!).

Use feathers, pipe cleaners, flowers, leaves, etc., to make this more fun.

Cut a strip of paper and tape it in a circle that fits your head. Decorate it with long strips like bunny ears!

Try this pizza hat! Cut a rubber band and attach each end to the side of a paper plate or large circle of cardboard. Decorate it like a pizza.

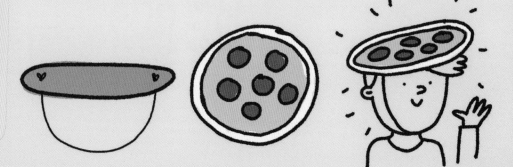

HAVE FUN WITH BUBBLE WRAP

Is it possible to NOT have fun with Bubble Wrap?! Here are a few ways:

The classic: just pop it!

Tap dance on it!

Wrap it around a paint roller and make a dot pattern!

Cut it in strips to make jellyfish.

Hang long strips from the top of your bedroom door to glam up the entrance.

MAKE A SUPERLONG DOMINO TRAIN

Try and use as many dominoes as you can to make a reeeeeeeally long domino train! Be careful not to knock them over before you're ready!

Try getting them to go down the stairs or around corners. That can be tricky but also a lot of fun.

BE CAREFUL NOT TO KNOCK THEM OVER!

ANOTHER FUN IDEA! Hack another common household game—playing cards! Build a playing card house like this:

DESIGN YOUR OWN
WEIRD FOOD

Today we're not settling for typical boring food on our shelves. Let's make up our own.

Collect empty food boxes (like from cereal). Carefully, completely open the boxes. Try not to rip the tabs that hold the box together.

Use your glue stick to reassemble the boxes, but inside out. Now you've got a great canvas to create some REALLY WEIRD FOOD PACKAGING!

A few ideas: Worm Puffs! Rock Soup! Macaroni & Sneeze!

MAKE MASKS

An easy way to make masks is with paper plates or a circle shape of cardboard with ribbons that are tied (or strips of paper that are taped) to hold it in place.

Use a hobby knife to cut holes for eyes.

Turn your mask into a bunny, a horse, a monster, a bug, or an alien!

PUT RIBBON ← HERE

ANOTHER FUN IDEA!
MAKE A CARDBOARD BOX SPACE HELMET!

BE A FAIRY
FOR A DAY

Fill an entire day with magic by wearing fancy wings.

What you'll need:

- Cardboard
- Pencil
- Scissors
- Ribbons
- Hole punch (or help from a parent)
- Paint, markers, and shiny materials to decorate

Steps:

1. Lay out a large sheet of cardboard and use a pencil to draw a shape like this:

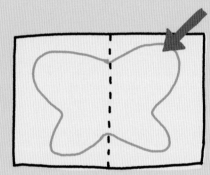

2. Cut it out, and fold it in half.

3. Use paint, markers, and collage to decorate the wings.

4. When they're dry, punch four holes in the wings, like this:

5. Push ribbon strips through the holes and tie them over your shoulders.

BE A SUPERHERO FOR A DAY

What is your superpower? What is your weakness? Who is your archnemesis? Choose your hero name, and now all you need is a cape!

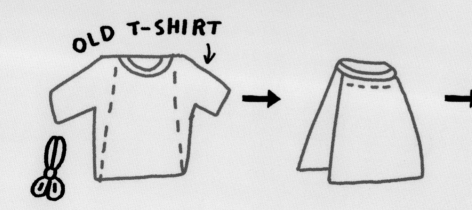

OLD T-SHIRT

ADD A MASK

DON'T FORGET TO DECORATE YOUR CAPE

Be sure to add your superhero logo. You can draw it on with fabric markers or puffy paint.

MAKE A MEMORY GAME

Cut 20 same-sized squares out of cardboard or any heavy paper (3 x 3 inches is a great size). Draw different objects on 10 of the cards, and then draw the SAME objects on the other 10 cards to make pairs. Make them as goofy as you'd like!

Mix them up and place them all facedown.

Turn over one at a time and try to find the matching card. Good luck remembering which image is where!

ANOTHER FUN IDEA! Instead of drawing two of the same objects, you can also draw two images that belong together. Like a grown animal and its baby, a fish and a fishbowl, a baseball and a bat, a foot and a sock, and so on. This makes a great present!

DO A CRAZY MANICURE

Trace your hands on cardboard and cut them out.
Use a small brush and acrylic paint to decorate the nails.

OOH! FANCY!

ADD JEWELRY TOO!

Or cut out your hand shape and make one of these:

PARTY
ON THE
COMPUTER!

Getting together virtually on the computer is just as much fun as a party at your house— without as much cleanup afterward.

PLAN A VIRTUAL PARTY

Choose a theme for your party! Here are a few ideas:

COSTUME PARTY

You can celebrate Halloween any month of the year. Dress up like your favorite monsters or even a character from a TV show or game.

STAND-UP COMEDY NIGHT

WHY WAS 6 AFRAID OF 7?

BECAUSE 7, 8, 9!

Get everyone to memorize three jokes (you can use notecards if you'd like!), and then take turns telling them.

TALENT SHOW

LA LA LAAA!

Show off your hidden skills at a VIRTUAL TALENT show! Get everyone to pick something they can do during the performance. Sing a song! Do a dance! Show off your karate skills! Or even jump rope!

CROSSWORD NIGHT

ANYONE KNOW 8 DOWN?

Find a good crossword puzzle online and send it to everyone before the party starts so that they can print it out. Work together to solve the puzzle. Want an extra challenge? Set a timer and see if you can beat the clock!

DIG DEEPER: Did you know that you can even do escape rooms online? Yep! Some companies offer virtual escape rooms that you can do with friends and family anywhere in the world.

DESIGN AN OLD-FASHIONED INVITE

Send out good old-fashioned snail mail invitations. Everyone likes to get mail! Be sure to include when the party is and how to connect.

You can also send an electronic invitation. Don't forget to add all the details!

DEAR _____ (FRIEND'S NAME)

YOU'RE INVITED TO A VIRTUAL PARTY!

WHEN _____

HOW TO LOG IN _____

IF YOU CAN MAKE IT, EMAIL ME!

_____ (YOUR EMAIL)

PLAY VIRTUAL GAMES

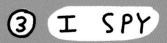
Here are a few fun things you can do with friends over the computer!

① SHOW-AND-TELL

Show off one of your favorite things in your house.

② TIC-TAC-TOE

A classic.

③ I SPY

Can you guess what your friend sees?

④ WOULD YOU RATHER

Everyone can share one of their favorites. You can also do a "Try-not-to-laugh Challenge." Take turns telling jokes and see who can hold in their laughter the longest.

WOULD YOU RATHER...

EAT A BEAN MILKSHAKE?

— OR —

KISS A JELLYFISH?

PET AN ALLIGATOR?

— OR —

WALK BAREFOOT IN MUD?

WALK ACROSS A DESERT?

— OR —

SWIM IN WATER WITH PIRAÑAS?

INVITE FRIENDS ON VIRTUAL OUTINGS

Believe it or not, LOTS of national parks, museums, and galleries have created VIRTUAL access to their sites and collections.

Sign on and take a tour together and talk about what you see. If you could go anywhere in the world, where would it be? Who would you take with you? What would you pack?

Where can you go? Into a volcano, to a mummy's tomb, even inside a Scottish castle!

VOLCANO

MUMMY'S TOMB

SCOTTISH CASTLE

HOLD A VIRTUAL TRIVIA NIGHT

Get to know your friends better with a good old-fashioned trivia night. You can play against each other or play as a team and try to get the highest score possible.

Find questions by looking up "trivia for kids." **Tip:** Don't just pick one topic! Maybe YOU love all things about one popular TV show . . . but there's a chance someone else has never even seen it! So stick to general trivia.

If you're all playing together as one team, have one person volunteer to write out your answers.

ANOTHER FUN IDEA! Have everyone coming bring two questions on a common theme (your town, family, local sports team, the weather). Take turns posing the questions to the group.

START A VIRTUAL BOOK CLUB WITH FRIENDS

Read the book beforehand and discuss it, or just take turns reading out loud. Grandparents, aunts, and uncles love book clubs, too.

NAME THAT SOUND

Find a website or a CD with lots of random sound effects on it. Play a sound and have everyone write down what they think it is. Once everyone has written their answers, compare them to see who was right.

It sounds easy, but trust me, it's not! Is that thunder or a growling jaguar?

SOUND EFFECTS

NAME THAT DOODLE

CAT

CHEESE

BANANA

BIKE

BAT

What you'll need:

- Anything to draw on! (it could be a dry-erase board or a large drawing tablet)
- Something to draw with

Create a set of cards with words that would be easy to draw (like *cat, dog, jumping, rain*). Decide whose turn it is to draw and have all of the other participants close their eyes. Have one person draw a card from the pile and show it to the artist (no peeking!). As the artist is drawing, try to guess what it is. The first to guess correctly gets a point. You can play in teams if you want.

FAMILY FUN!

Movie nights!

Indoor camping!

Spa day!

This section is loaded with stuff the entire family can do together!

HAVE A PAJAMA DAY

Eat breakfast food for every meal.

Do something outside in your pajamas.

Make slippers out of tissue boxes.

Read bedtime stories in the morning.

Eat lunch on your bed (only if parents say okay!).

ENJOY STORIES TOGETHER

- Read together. Find a book that fits all ages, and take turns reading to each other.
- There are lots of great podcasts and audiobooks that are perfect for the whole family. Pick a topic that you all enjoy and listen.

FAMILY DISCUSSION: People make podcasts about topics they know a lot about. What would your podcast be about?

DO A PUZZLE TOGETHER

This one is a classic way to hang out with family. Be sure to pick a puzzle that's great for even the youngest helper.

THROW A FAMILY GAME NIGHT

Set out several games and vote on what to play first. Or learn a classic card game like rummy, spoons, or whist.

TIP: It's always fun to trade board games or puzzles with your neighbors. Also, some libraries have games to check out.

PLAY A GUESSING GAME

Write the name of an animal, object, food, or famous person on pieces of paper. Tape one to each person's forehead so they can't see it (and don't peek at yours!). Go around in a circle trying to guess the word on your forehead by asking yes-or-no questions. If the answer is yes, ask again. If the answer is no, it's the next person's turn.

SANDWICH

PUT ON A FASHION SHOW

HAT
GLASSES
SCARF
BANGLES
BAG
BIG SHIRT
DAD'S WATCH
BELT
MOM'S SHOES

You can either work with the clothes that you have, or try and design a few new pieces. Don't forget scarves, sunglasses, and hats. Maybe someone in the house owns some fancy shoes you can borrow. Include a special hairdo, makeup, and music. Practice your strut!

OTHER FUN IDEAS!
- Kids dress a parent!
- Kids dress as a parent!
- Vote for your favorite outfits.
- Give your creation a name.

HAVE AN AIR GUITAR COMPETITION

Everyone picks a song with a great guitar solo and competes to have the funniest, coolest, most impressive performance.

SING KARAOKE

Find free karaoke sites online! Use a hairbrush as a pretend microphone, OR find a wireless one that will connect to your computer.

CAMP INSIDE

- If your family has a tent, set it up inside! If not, use a big sheet to make your own.

- Set up a speaker to play nature sounds.

- Make s'mores in the kitchen over the stove and enjoy them in your tent.

- Sleep in sleeping bags, or use your blankets and pillows from your bed.

SHEET

CHAIRS

ANOTHER FUN IDEA!
Hang a clothesline across the room with a sheet draped over it. Use books to weigh down the sides.

FAMILY DISCUSSION!
Where would you go on a vacation? Would you be scared to camp out in the dark? What would you be nervous about?

HAVE A SPA DAY

A few easy spa day classics you can do at home:

Soak your feet in the bath with soap.

Paint each other's nails.

Slice a cucumber and put them over your eyes for 5 minutes.

Make a smoothie with veggies, berries, and your favorite juice.

Make your own lip gloss.

Try a bath bomb!

Try a face mask.

To make lip gloss:

1. Scoop 3 spoonfuls of petroleum jelly into a small bowl, and microwave it for 1 minute or until it's liquidy. If it hasn't melted after one minute, keep microwaving, a little bit at a time, and stir when you check on it.

2. Take it out and mix in half a pack of powdered fruit punch (like Kool-Aid).

3. Let it cool, and you've got your own homemade lip gloss!

You don't need a fancy face mask to make your skin feel great!
Banana face mask: Mash up a ripe banana. Spread it on your face (stay clear of your eyes!). Relax for 10–20 minutes. Rinse with cold water.

HOLD FAMILY OLYMPICS

Have a week without any plans at all? Why not hold your own Olympics? Have a few competitions each day! Make medals for the winners!

Possible competitions:

- Cornhole
- Ring toss
- Races around the house
- Races down the block
- Relay races
- Hopping races
- Interpretive dance
- Kick the most soccer goals in one minute

See who can do these the longest:

- Stand on one foot
- Plank
- Hold their arms out to the sides
- Balance a pillow on their head
- Hold something heavy
- Hold their breath
- Stare into another's eyes without blinking
- Jump rope without missing
- Keep a balloon in the air

PLAN THE ULTIMATE
MOVIE NIGHT

There's nothing more totally awesome than a family movie night. Be sure to take movie suggestions from the whole family and then vote on it.

- Have snack foods that fit the theme of the movie night.

- Draw a poster to announce this week's movie night theme and hand out tickets to everyone in the family.

- Dress like the characters when you watch.

- Make snacks inspired by the setting of the movie or something they eat in the film.

- Make your own movie festival! Pick a few movies that all fit together in some way. Maybe they all have one actor in different roles. Maybe it's a movie that has a part 2 and 3. Watch them all in one weekend!

NOW PLAYING
MAGICAL NANNY
THE MOVIE

WHEN: TONIGHT @ 6PM
WHERE: the living room
DRESS CODE: PAJAMAS!

DRAW A FAMILY TREE

Talk with your parents, grandparents, aunts—anyone in the family—and try to make the biggest family tree you can! Start by just making notes, and then when you've collected as many names as you can, draw a GREAT BIG POSTER! Do you know who your great-grandparents were? Did your grandmother have a sister? Try to get your family to send photos of everyone or draw their portraits.

MAKE A FAMILY SCRAPBOOK

- Put a photo of one person on a page in a blank book or sketchbook.

- Interview your family members and ask them to tell you some of their favorite things about that person or memories of them, and write them down. Don't forget to call and ask people who live far away.

- Take turns writing down some of your favorite stories about the people in your family, like how Granny loves to drive a motorcycle!

PLACES SHE'S LIVED

PLACES SHE'S WORKED

PETS SHE'S OWNED

FAVORITE THINGS TO EAT

HOBBIES

NANNY

FAVORITE VACATION

OUTSIDE ADVENTURES!

Find some new bugs and maybe even meet a fairy!
This section will get you out of the house
and loving the great outdoors.

MAKE A BIRD FEEDER

YUM!

WITH A PINECONE! Spread peanut butter on a pinecone and roll it in birdseed. Hang it from a tree with twine.

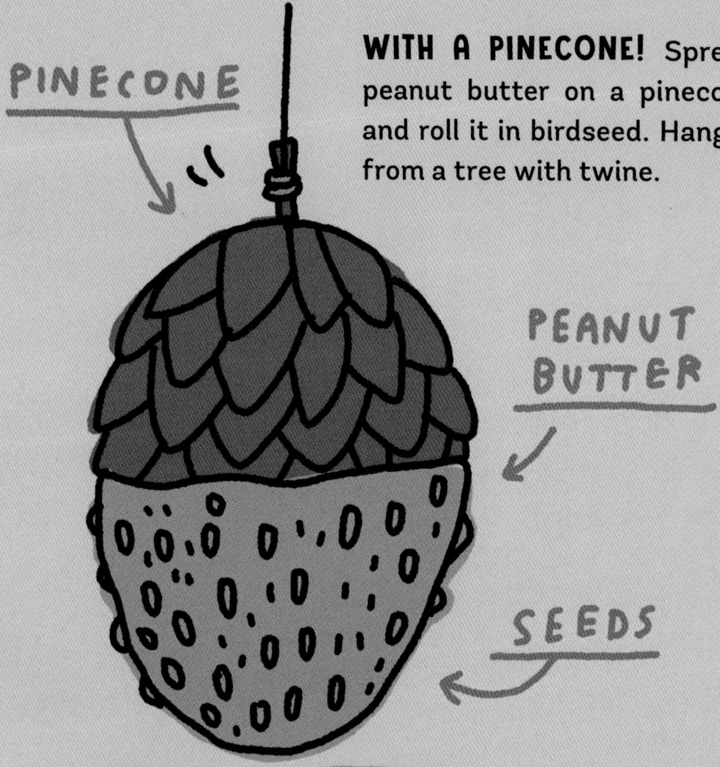

PINECONE

PEANUT BUTTER

SEEDS

YUM!

TWINE

MILK CARTON

SEED

WITH A (CLEAN) MILK CARTON! Cut a hole in the side big enough for a bird and fill the bottom of the carton with birdseed. Decorate it and hang it outside with twine.

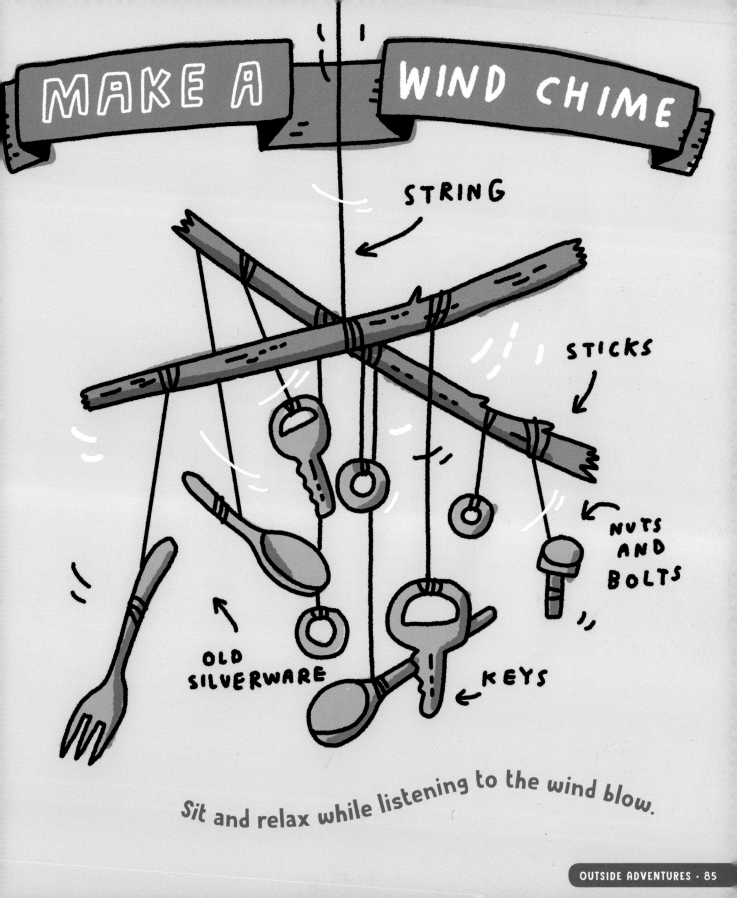

MAKE A WIND CHIME

STRING

STICKS

NUTS AND BOLTS

OLD SILVERWARE

KEYS

Sit and relax while listening to the wind blow.

CREATE A FAIRY GARDEN

Fairies love to have a little place to hang out, so let's build one for them!

You can make a fairy garden in a pot or dish, or you can build it directly into a flower bed in your backyard.

- Start with a shallow pot or dish.

- Fill with a thin layer of topsoil or potting soil (2–4 inches deep).

- Arrange plants (a few options: moss, succulents, small flowering plants).

- Add flat rocks as paths for the fairies to walk on.

- Add small benches, chairs, and even a little house! (You can get these from your dollhouse or at any place that sells model train houses.)

- Add worms (optional).

- Still feeling crafty? Get some modeling clay, mold it into mushroom shapes, and bake in the oven.

DIG DEEPER: Look at pictures of fairy gardens to get inspired. Become the next famous fairy-garden architect!

MAKE A SUNDIAL

Before phones had clocks on them, people had to use . . . well, clocks! And before clocks, there were sundials to help people tell time. They're fun to make and easy to use.

1. Find a sunny spot outside that will be undisturbed for a few days. Collect 12 rocks that are about the same size.

2. Start early in the morning and stand up a stick (approximately 2 feet long) in the ground.

3. At the turn of the next hour, place a rock where the end of the stick's shadow falls. Mark the time on the rock. For one day, every hour on the hour, go and put a rock where the shadow falls.

4. Go out the next day and check the time!

MAKE A NATURE MAP

Make a map of your yard, garden, or neighborhood. If there are plants you don't know, look them up and add them to your map. You can also include doghouses, certain trees, neighbors' houses, and other fun stuff!

OTHER FUN IDEAS!

Outdoor bingo: Make a bingo sheet with items that you can see and find outside, like a bird, a bug, a rock, a flower, a tree, a hill, a cloud, or a fire hydrant.

Scavenger hunt: Plan a scavenger hunt in your backyard or the park, writing clues that will lead people to specific spots and hiding them in different locations. Hide a prize at the end.

Easter egg hunt: It doesn't have to be Easter eggs. Take 5 items and hide them in your backyard or at a park. Get someone else in your family to come find them.

PLANT A GARDEN

Planting a garden is a great activity to do with an adult. Have them help you pick a good spot to plant a few things.

MAKE A WINDOW GARDEN

Great flowers, herbs, vegetables . . . even spicy peppers can grow really well near a sunny window.

You can use a large fish tank, a long plastic planting box, or lots of little flower pots, whatever is easier.

Don't forget to label what you're growing with little signs.

A few easy things to grow include mint, rosemary, scallions, and wildflowers.

BLOW GIANT BUBBLES

TWIST TIES

ROPE

STICK

WASHER

BUBBLE SOLUTION

What you'll need:

- Bubble solution:
  - 6 cups water
  - 1 cup dishwashing soap
  - ½ cup cornstarch
  - 2 tablespoons baking powder
  - 2 tablespoons corn syrup
  - 3 feet of long, thick rope
- 1 metal washer
- Small twist ties
- 2 dowel rods (2 feet long)

Steps:

1. Pour the bubble solution ingredients in a bucket and stir gently to mix.

2. Remove the top layer of foam.

3. Tie the rope in a big loop. Attach the washer to the ends of the knot.

4. Use the twist ties to attach the rope to the dowel rods.

5. Dip the rope into the bubble solution, spread the dowel rods, and wave through the air.

PLAY FRISBEE HORSESHOES

Who says you need real horseshoes to play horseshoes? Push two dowel rods (or sticks) into the ground, approximately 12 feet apart.

1. Choose a throwing spot.

2. Take turns throwing your Frisbees, trying to get them as close to the posts as you can. (Beanbags work, too!)

SCORING

- 5 points if your Frisbee is touching the post.

- 1 point for every Frisbee that is closer to the posts than your opponent's closest one.

BEANBAGS WORK GREAT! ✓

CANS OF BEANS DON'T! ✗

GO STARGAZING

Did you know that on a clear night, you can see around 2,000 stars in the sky without a telescope?

One of the best ways to look at stars now is by using fancy technology called AUGMENTED REALITY. But don't worry; you don't need to be a rocket scientist to make it work. Just download a stargazing app and point it toward the sky. Constellations, stars, and even planets will automatically be identified. Can you find the Big Dipper? What about Orion's belt?

START A BUG OR BIRD JOURNAL

What you'll need:

- A small lined journal or notebook
- Binoculars (optional)

Start keeping a record of all of the birds, bugs, and other wildlife you see outside of your window or when you go on walks. If you find a new animal, do some DIGGING to figure out what kind it is and add it to your book!

Draw the animals you see or print out pictures from online to add to your journal.

ANOTHER FUN IDEA!

Create your own bug and bird journal using your imagination. Picture a fantastical world in your mind. What is this world called? What do the animals look like in your fantasy world? What are their names? What do they like to eat and how do they live? Are they dangerous? Or are they cuddly little friends?

PAINT ROCKS

Find some cool-looking rocks and use acrylic paint to decorate them! You can use googly eyes to make them really silly.

Place some in your neighborhood to surprise people.

LEARN SOMETHING NEW!

It's time for an upgrade . . . for your BRAIN! This section features some suggestions for new things you can memorize and new skills that are fun to learn . . . and even more fun to show off!

LEARN ORIGAMI

Origami is the traditional art of paper folding. If it sounds hard, don't worry—you've already done it . . . when you made a paper airplane!

Don't have origami paper?! Not a problem! Lots of origami can be done using whatever paper you have around the house! You just have to make it square.

Let's start with an easy one!

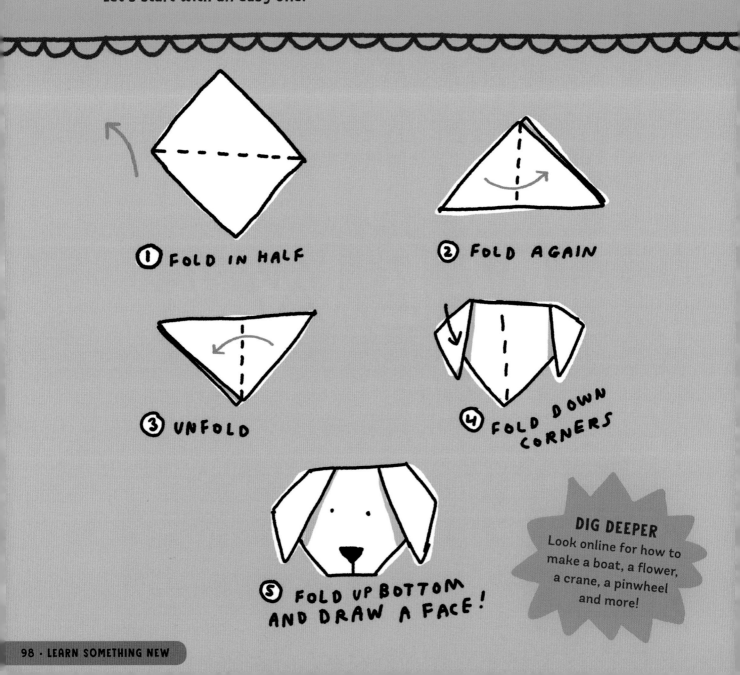

① FOLD IN HALF

② FOLD AGAIN

③ UNFOLD

④ FOLD DOWN CORNERS

⑤ FOLD UP BOTTOM AND DRAW A FACE!

DIG DEEPER
Look online for how to make a boat, a flower, a crane, a pinwheel and more!

MEMORIZE SOMETHING FUN

Have you ever had to memorize something for school? At first it might seem impossible, but the more you try to remember it, the easier it gets! And think of how many people you can impress with your knowledge!

A few things to try and memorize:

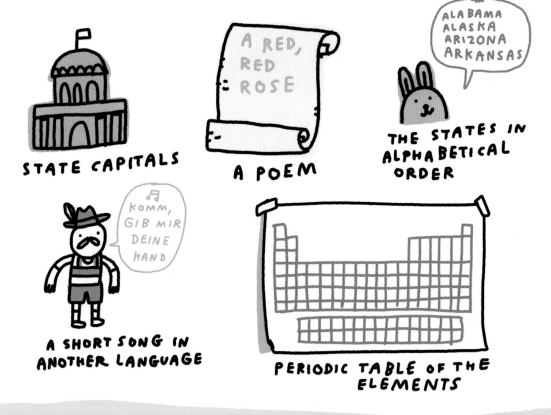

STATE CAPITALS

A RED, RED ROSE

A POEM

ALABAMA
ALASKA
ARIZONA
ARKANSAS

THE STATES IN ALPHABETICAL ORDER

KOMM, GIB MIR DEINE HAND

A SHORT SONG IN ANOTHER LANGUAGE

PERIODIC TABLE OF THE ELEMENTS

LEARN GREETINGS IN DIFFERENT LANGUAGES

This might come in handy if you ever get to take a trip around the world. And maybe you'll get to see some of the traditional clothing worn by different cultures, too!

BONJOUR
(BOHN-juhr)
French

¡HOLA!
(OH-lah)
Spanish

你好
(NǏ HĂO)
(nee-HOW)
Mandarin

مرحبا
MERHABA
(MER-ha-bah)
Turkish

こんにちは
(KONNICHIWA)
(koh-nee-chee-wah)
Japanese

GUTEN TAG!
(GOO-ten TAK)
German

नमस्ते
(NAMASTE)
(nah-MAH-stay)
Hindi

привет
(PRIVET)
(pree-VYET)
Russian

LEARN
AN
INSTRUMENT

Pick an instrument and learn a few basics!

Instruments can often be tough and take a long time to master, but it's not hard to get started. One favorite is the ukulele. It is small, and the strings are typically nylon, which makes it easier for small hands than a guitar. Go online and watch videos of how to play.

Here are some other instruments that are easy to learn:

HARMONICA

RECORDER

XYLOPHONE

DRUMS

UKULELE

LEARN SOME SIGN LANGUAGE

LEARN A magic TRICK

You don't need fancy magic props to learn a magic trick. You can use a deck of cards or even a few rubber bands.

THE FLOATING PENCIL.

① HOLD A PENCIL. ② OPEN YOUR HAND.

HOW it's DONE!

DIG DEEPER: Look up videos of easy magic tricks to do at home. The step-by-step tutorials are great, and the next time you hang out with friends, you'll be a magician!

MAKE A MASTERPIECE

Have you already made it all the way through this book and STILL need something fun to do? Okay! No problem! Here's an easy one: Make an artistic masterpiece!

Grab your favorite art supplies and just MAKE something!

Sculpt something with clay! Draw someone in your family! Draw your dream pet! Put all of that and more into one amazing piece!

Get the whole family involved and have a big art show. Serve little cups of juice and sliced cheese.

Play violin music on the computer, get dressed up, and walk around with your nose in the air.

Show off your masterpiece to everyone you can, and maybe the creativity will be contagious. There are endless activities to be discovered at home—have fun imagining more!